REVELATION
from
Creation

REVELATION
from
Creation

True Tales from the North Woods

CARL DIENER

Cover Art by my friend Kevin Moffat, Kevin@mannaart.com, Check out his work. Only God can paint a better sunset.

Publishing services by Selah Publishing Group, LLC, Tennessee. The views expressed or implied in this work do not necessarily reflect those of Selah Publishing Group.

ISBN: 978-1-58930-230-0
Library of Congress Control Number: 2009900743

Dedicated to my wife Laurie.

And my son Samuel,
who edited this book so it all made sense.

Contents

Introduction

This book is just a few stories of things that happened to me in and around the woods and the things that God taught me about them. A fine young preacher and evangelist by the name of Gary Morgan told me I should make a book out of them. He thought they were a great blessing. I hope you will find them to be a blessing as well.

Carl Diener

Carl Diener

Wee Little Rodents and the Love of God

> If ye then, being evil, know how to give
> good gifts unto your children, how much
> more shall your Father in heaven give good
> things to them that ask him?
> GOSPEL OF ST. MATTHEW, CHAPTER 7 VERSE 11

Every spring my wife Laurie and I would pack up the truck and we'd take a trip up north to camp out for a few days. At the place we camp there isn't a house or electricity for 20 miles. At night with only the light of a campfire you can see the roof that God made; billions and billions of stars. You can see the milky way in all its glory (with no city lights to block it out), all of it declaring the grandeur and splendor of our God. He made it all, the awesome beauty of it, the trees and the mountains, the vastness of it! The wonder of it! Sometimes when I'm out there the joy of the Lord just hits me to think my Dad made all of this beauty for me to live in.

The beauty of off-season camping is that there are no other people around, no cars, no radios, no street sounds. All you can hear are the sounds of the world He made. The wind blowing in the trees at night, the rush of the stream, and the cry of a loon. Of course it's cold in the early spring in a tent. If you have a wife, get yourselves a sleeping bag for two. The cold at night will give you both a reason to snuggle up close. I don't know if you need a reason for that, but there it is.

It was on one such camping trip that God showed me something that I will never forget. I was sitting by the campfire having a cup of hot coffee when I noticed a little flash of brown rushing around the campsite. I watched carefully and saw that it was a tiny field mouse. He would dash out and grab a crumb of fallen food before darting back into the safety of the grass. I watched him for about five minutes and discovered he was taking the food to his burrow next to a big rock about five yards from the stream bank.

Well, that gave me an idea. I thought, "I'm gonna bless that little mouse's socks off." Now we always take a lot of food camping. I have a big cook-box I made that fits on the tailgate of our 4x4 truck. The side of the box folds open and makes a food preparation surface. In the box are shelves for pots and pans, canned food, bread, oatmeal, sugar, coffee, tea, salt, pepper, and anything else you would have in the kitchen. Also we have a cooler for eggs, bacon, milk and all that stuff. There's plenty to spare.

The next thing the mouse saw when he popped out of his hole was a giant pile of oatmeal. He stopped and he sniffed and he took a little bite. He couldn't believe what he was seeing; he just stood there trembling with excitement. Soon, however, he was carrying pawfuls down his hole. And guess what? He'd gone and woke up little mum mouse and she was helping too. So all morning I blessed them just for the fun of seeing their little furry faces all excited. The mountain of oatmeal was replaced with a mountain of marshmallows which they rolled down their hole, then bread, nuts, hot dog roll bits and goodness knows what else I set out for them. The funniest was a plastic spoon loaded with peanut butter. The little mouse ran out and grabbed the spoon, and *clunk* he got the spoon crosswise of the hole. Finally he stopped and thought, and then fed the thing end first down the hole. A few minutes later out popped the spoon without the peanut butter.

About that time I heard the Lord speak to my heart. "You, for the pleasure of seeing that mouse blessed, have poured out more than the little fellow could have ever dreamed of or imagined, just on a whim. How much more do you think I enjoy pouring out my blessings on my children who I dearly love?" That really touched me. We spend so much of our lives fearfully grabbing for the crumbs that fall. Oh, to grab hold of His heart for us! Let's turn our beady little eyes toward heaven and let Him show us how he feels about us.

Talkin Hawk

But even the very hairs of your head are numbered. Fear not therefore: ye are of more value than many sparrows.

GOSPEL OF ST. LUKE, CHAPTER 12 VERSE 7

One fine sunny early summer day I was out in the chaise lounge, looking up at the clear blue sky and just telling the Lord what a good job he did making it all. To top off the beauty of that summer morning, high in the sky was a pair of Redtail hawks soaring in the warm summer thermal. They have a very distinctive cry, and it occurred to me that I could do a fair imitation of it. So I gave it a try, but I did not get any response.

Well, I got so I would drop whatever I was doing when I heard their cry and walk outside just for the sheer wonder of watching those beautiful birds soaring high in the air. And yes, each time I would do my best to give them a call back on their shrill cries. I don't know when it first happened, but one day I gave a good whistle and one of the hawks replied. To my surprise he came right down and landed on the big beech tree that overhangs our deck. He perched there for quite a while. We had a "conversation" and then finally he took to soaring again. Heck, I was thrilled.

"I bet that won't happen again," I thought to myself. Still, the next time I heard the hawks calling to one another I had to go out and try again. This time I heard them far over the ridge. I gave a call and one hawk soared over the house calling back to me. Sure enough, it was my friend, a young juvenile redtail. He soared down and landed again on that same branch of the old beech tree. Again we had an exchange. He would give his shrill call and then tip his head to wait and hear my response. After a while he would take off again, soaring high above the ridge. It began to be a regular morning routine. I would go out on the deck and give the shrill whistle of the red tail, and from near or far away, he would come soaring above the treetops to land for our "talk".

When I skipped a few mornings I would eventually hear my wife asking for me in the early morning: "Your friend is out on the beach tree calling for you!" Sure enough, he was perched there whistling for me until I came out. We would have our talk and again he would take off.

One bright sunny warm morning, I was still in bed and Laurie called me out to the deck. I got out of bed with nothing on but my jockey shorts and walked out on the deck. (We live way out in the woods; there's no people to see me.) I gave him a whistle and then another one but he just stared at me. My wife said to me something like, "Maybe you should go inside and put on some feathers, if you know what I mean." I went into the house and put my shirt and overalls on and came out again. I gave him another whistle and he responded happily. Yes, I thought, I guess it's kind of a shock to see your friend plucked clean.

Well, the time soon came when he no longer came by or answered when I called him. I guess he grew up and maybe adult hawks can't see any sense in talking to humans. And perhaps adult humans should have better things to do than make friends with hawks. Yet I enjoyed our friendship very much and I missed it.

Come to think of it, I can't imagine why the great God, the creator of heaven and earth, the one that spoke the stars into existence, would want to talk with humans either. However, he does in fact seem to enjoy our companionship. So much so that he sent his only son to visit us here on earth. You know the price He paid so that we could be God's friend. He hung on a cross.

The next summer I was walking in the wood and I heard the cry of a red tail hawk. I gave an answering call. The hawk followed me home, going from tree to tree until I arrived on my deck. He landed a final time on the limb of the old beech tree where my friend used to perch and then he took off. Maybe he was my old friend. I would like to think so.

Carl Diener

Where the Beaver live

> He that believeth on me, as the scripture
> hath said, out of his belly shall flow rivers
> of living water.
>
> THE GOSPEL ACCORDING TO ST. JOHN CHAPTER 7 VERSE 38

In the north country of New Hampshire, you can find places where the beaver have no restrictions or manmade obstacles. Here they are free to use the largest streams and work them as they like. The results of their efforts are some of the most amazing examples of animal ingenuity you will find.

One winter day I took a long hike to just such a place, where there was an actual river that had been dammed by a family of beavers. The air was crisp and cold and the sky overcast, with a hint of more snow falling soon. When I got there I found the pond frozen over solidly enough to walk on. Most of the existing snow seemed to have been wind-blown off the surface and I found I had little trouble walking out to the middle of the pond where the beavers' lodge was. The top of the lodge was also free of snow and you could see the wisp of vapor from the warm moist air wafting up from within the lodge through the vent hole. You see, every beaver lodge has to have a vent hole because the only way to get in or out of the lodge is by swimming underwater. Without a vent, the beavers couldn't breathe.

As I looked more closely at the top of the lodge I could see signs of some type of predator, perhaps a coyote or wildcat. It appeared that the animal had been driven mad by the scent of possible prey coming from the vent hole, and had attempted the impossible task of digging through the lodge to the beavers inside. Of course, whoever it was, they had to give it up as a bad job. It is impossible to break through a beaver lodge in winter without the assistance of, say, several sticks of dynamite. The wood and mud lodge walls are frozen solid to a layer of several feet thick. The place is completely impregnable to any ordinary predator.

Beavers are a truly unique mammal. More than any other, they have made the rivers and flowing streams their home. Jesus said that when the Spirit came, out of our innermost being would flow rivers of living water. It says in the Old Testament that there is a river that makes glad the city of God. Friends, there still is a river of the Spirit of God and we can live there. As I was standing next to that beaver family's home it became so clear how the Lord intended us to live. The beaver has found life, strength, and safety in the river. He knows how, when, and where to make the banks overflow. When he makes a dam he is not stopping the flow of the river, he is simply creating a greater place for it to fill. The flow in to his pond still equals the flow out over the dam. Yet, because of the dam, there is more water that he can live and work in.

Have you ever seen where a beaver has cut down a great tree and there is nothing left but the gnawed-off stump? You might wonder how such a small animal could haul away such a huge tree. Well, look around. You'll see the dam has caused the water's edge to be only a few feet from the base of the stump. All the beaver had to do was cut the tree off so it fell into the water. Then the beaver, with very little effort, could float it to the place where he wanted it, making his dam even larger. So you see how the relatively weak beaver used the rising water level to his advantage. The water supported the weight of the work. We as Christians ought to be thinking of ways to cause the water level of the Holy Spirit to rise in our lives so that the work we do will be supernaturally supported. It is the Spirit that does the heavy lifting.

In the waters of the ever-flowing river, the beaver has made a reservoir. He finds his safety and security in it and never strays far from the waters. Here is a lesson for us to stay in the Spirit's flow. It is in the river of God we can find safety. Here he can reach us and we can hear his voice.

I once was hiking along a lonely stretch of a good-sized stream above a beaver dam. It was another cold winter day and it was snowing at the time. When I stopped to rest the stillness was like nothing you can experience anywhere near human habitation. There was no wind, not even a breeze. The only sound was the quiet gurgling of the stream under the ice.

Out of the corner of my eye I saw a slight motion and turned to see that a beaver had slipped down the bank of the stream not more than ten feet from me. Beavers eat the bark of willow and poplar and young birch, and this one had a small piece of poplar branch in his mouth. I don't know what had caused him to venture out into the cold that day; perhaps he had tired of his winter store of cuttings or even simply run out.

He stood there looking at me for a few moments with a total lack of fear. You see, the water, his source of life and safety, was only a foot away. In a flash the beaver vanished through a hole in the ice. One moment he was there, seemingly vulnerable, the next he was gone. He was gone below the surface, lost to the dangers of the world, far beneath the laughing waters of that beautiful stream.

Run for the River

There is a river, the streams whereof shall make glad the city of God, the holy place of the tabernacles of the most High. God is in the midst of her; she shall not be moved: God shall help her and that right early.

PSALMS 46 VERSES 4 & 5

Raccoons don't have any serious enemies anymore, except for man. Man alone is not much of a problem unless he is hunting a raccoon with dogs. A man with a set of dogs is a deadly combination for any coon. Unlike a fox, the coon can never outrun a dog. Many of them will take to the trees, where the man following the dogs simply has to shoot them down.

But a wise old coon will make sure he is never far from a body of water, preferably a river. When he hears the hounds are after him and he knows he is in trouble, he heads straight for the water. He knows once he reaches it and dives in the water his enemy will loose the scent. The hounds won't be able to track him anymore; the current of the river will carry him far away, leaving them yammering on the shore.

The smartest coons know another thing about their enemy. The hounds are not very good swimmers. Sometimes a coon will swim out to deep water and wait until the hounds arrive. He will let the dogs see him, and when they swim out after him the coon will dive, come up behind one of the dogs, climb up its back and hang on till the dog drowns. Then he does the same to the next dog.

One day when we were worshiping in a church service, singing about the river, I felt the Lord remind me of this. We should all have the sense of an old coon to run for the river and dive in. In the river of God there is freedom from the cares of the world and the enemies that pursue us. In the river of the flow of God's Spirit there is the anointing to turn the tables on our enemy, to put him under our feet until he doesn't come up anymore.

Carl Diener

Stay in the Light Unless....

I am like a pelican of the wilderness: I am
like an owl of the desert.
PSALM 102 VERSE 6

The Bible tells us that when we were born again,
we were taken out of the kingdom of darkness into the
kingdom of his marvelous light. It also tells us that
we should walk in the light. But what if you are an
owl? Well, God made the owls to live in the dark. If
there were a Bible written for owls it would tell them
to walk (or rather fly) in the dark, because in the day
they are almost blinded by the bright sunlight. The
best thing for an owl is to find a nice thick pine and
stay there in the day, then come out and hunt in the
night. However, like some Christians, there are owls
that feel they are missing out and start moving outside
of their element. They go out before nightfall and they
get themselves into trouble.

One time I was in my tree stand about two hours
before dark when I heard a large flock of blue jays.
Their harsh cries were getting louder as they came
closer. Soon I heard a rustle of leaves and a thump as
a great owl crash-landed on a tree branch not far from
me. In a matter of minutes the flock of jays descended
through the leaves. They began screaming and diving

on the poor owl, who perched helplessly on the branch, blinking stupidly and ducking the painful stabs of the jays' beaks.

So what happened? Well, the owl must have been caught in the daylight by the jays. They found no end of delight in baiting their enemy while he was at a disadvantage. That poor owl was miserable and in a great deal of pain. His torment would be long because it was still two hours before dark. What a sight! If it was dark, the great owl would be the king of the night sky and any jays caught napping by him would have no chance. Yet here he was in pain and at the mercy of the jays, who showed him none.

Why are so many Christians so miserable? Maybe it's because they are still moving around outside of their element, which is the light. Maybe it's because there are still areas of darkness where the enemy finds that they are vulnerable to his torment. If we stay in the light as He is in the light, we can soar higher and rest easier, free from much of what ails us.

How Squirrels Drive Me Nuts, and a Chipmunk That Found a Home

> Yea, the sparrow hath found an house,
> and the swallow a nest for herself, where
> she may lay her young, even thine altars,
> O Lord of hosts, my King and my God.
> PSALMS 84 VERSE 3

I find rodents in general to be a most interesting part of God's creation. When it comes to the rodent family, it seems obvious that they never read the book of Genesis. They think it is all about them multiplying and taking dominion over the earth. It never occurs to them that the dominion of the earth is supposed to belong to us two-legged creatures, or that we don't build houses and garages just for them to live in and cupboards to store food for them to eat. It's the same with the wild rodents of the forest. The beaver thinks he can build a dam down in Massachusetts and make a nice pond for himself; never mind the fact that he also fills the basements of half a dozen houses with water. If you tried to explain to him that this is wrong, he would not understand. After all, from his point of view every good home is built on water. If your home is flooded when he makes his pond, he has done you a favor. In addition, the state of Massachusetts was kind enough to ban leg hold traps. So beavers have little to fear from their waterlogged two-legged neighbors.

The red squirrels and chipmunks of the woods exhibit a similar lack of respect for God's higher authority in creation. It is with great trepidation that I sit waiting in my tree stand or on the forest floor when there are lots of red squirrels around. The idea when hunting deer is to sit or move quietly enough so that you remain unnoticed until you are able to sight your game and take it down. This is not possible if you happen to be spotted by a red squirrel. I've seen it happen time and again. The squirrel sees you sitting there and wonders what that large motionless object is doing in his woods. He does not remember this thing being there before. So he drops the nut he was chewing on and runs in for a closer look. The game has now started. You better not move a muscle or blink an eye, especially if you happen to be sitting in a tree stand when hunting. If you can remain motionless long enough for the red squirrel to go back to its day's activities you are safe. However, if the squirrel gets close enough to make the startling discovery that there is a human sitting in a tree, the chattering and the scolding begins. No one has been able to translate squirrel language but I imagine they are saying something like:

"Look, all you forest creatures, there is a human sitting in this tree! Better watch out, humans sitting in trees are up to no good. What are you doing in that tree, human? Hey all you deer within the sound of my voice, do you know why a human would sit in a tree? Bad human! You should go home; trees are for squirrels."

The scolding can go on for quite a while. Long enough, at least, that any passing deer would know something was up.

Then there is the other problem that can happen with squirrels or chipmunks. I suppose it has to do with the fall of Adam. The event seems to have corrupted all of creation to some degree. Far from living in bliss and harmony, the squirrels seem to have adapted the fallen human trait of the domestic squabble. They are quite ready to take to fighting and chasing each other. Thus, if you happen to be a hapless human sitting on the forest floor or in a tree or leaning on one, and you find yourself in the way of the chase, you will not be treated with respect as God's higher form of creation. You are very likely to get run over.

Many times I have heard one red squirrel chasing another down the tree I happen to be sitting in or using as a back-rest. I can hear the frantic scampering getting closer and closer. If I jump out of the way, I will have two irate squirrels turning their attention to scolding me for startling them. The best thing I can do is brace myself for the uncomfortable feeling of being treated as so much tree bark, while the two of them continue their spiral chase down the tree trunk and over my body. Fortunately I wear heavy wool clothing during the fall season. Still, there is nothing that can quite match the sensation of two very active scrambling squirrels tearing around your torso and down your leg, using the toe of your boot as a launching pad. The good thing is that the experience lasts only a second or two.

One of the many parallel activities associated with hunting is finding a place for my thermos of hot soup while eating lunch. People have no idea how hard it is to find a stable place on a forest floor all uneven with sticks and leaves and such. The floor of the woods was not made to stand long cylindrical things on end. Numerous times I have thought I found a good place to stand my thermos only to find it tipped over when I wasn't looking.

This fall I was sitting there enjoying my lunch when, you guessed it, I spotted two squirrels having a grand chase; and of course they were headed right for where my thermos was balanced precariously on a pile of forest litter. Having your body run over is bad enough but I was not about to sacrifice my soup. I made a lunge for it just in time to save it from being pitched into the leaves. Of course the hindmost squirrel spotted me and the scolding began:

"Bad human! What are you doing in my woods clutching steaming round cylindrical things?" and so on.

My encounters with the rodent family aren't limited to my hunting expeditions. One particular chipmunk happened to cross my deck frequently on his commute to wherever the heck the little guy was going in such a hurry every day. For some reason I took a liking to the little fellow and began leaving cookies and crackers and bits of bread out for him on his run. My wife and I very much enjoyed watching him stop for a brief repast on his way to wherever he was going. It was not long before he took to hanging around for further handouts and discovered that the bright red tomatoes in old dad's potted tomato plant tasted as good to him as they did to old dad. So then it became a race for me to pick them just before they became ripe and put them in a cardboard box just inside the kitchen door to ripen so I could eventually make a salad for my own enjoyment.

Well, one day my wife Laurie left the screen door ajar. When she came back into the kitchen she found that the chipmunk had gotten in and discovered where all his tasty red tomatoes had gone. Right there in mid tomato their eyes met. Laurie responded in typical female human fashion by emitting a high pitched shriek.

The chipmunk, finding himself greatly outsized, made good his escape at high speed. Laurie told me in no uncertain terms that while the chipmunk was cute outside, we could not have him coming in the house. Well, this is true and I have an interesting theological point to make with this whole episode. The old creature we were before we came to Jesus could not be allowed to come into the heavenly Father's house no matter how cute we were. We had to become new creatures, as the Bible explains, through the new birth. If the chipmunk were to become reborn as a human it could come into our house. So you see, as new creatures in Christ we are now welcome in the house of our heavenly father.

Though, come to think of it, if Laurie came into the kitchen and found a strange human eating the tomatoes the reaction would probably have been the same as with the chipmunk. But that is beside the point.

One day when I went down the back steps of the deck I found that our chipmunk friend had dug a cozy hole right next to my back step. The little fellow had showed more sense than many Christians do. After all, our heavenly Father takes care of us, loves us so much, and rescues us from so many situations. You would think we would want to make our home in his presence; but we spend so much of our day away from home, with our minds on other things, taken up with worry or activities, until we forget about him.

The psalmist remarks about how the swallows loved to come and nest around God's altar. Perhaps we too should learn to make our home right there in his presence, where there is fullness of joy and we find true pleasures forevermore.

Carl Diener

Tadpoles

And God made the beast of the earth after his kind, and cattle after their kind, and every thing that creepeth upon the earth after his kind: and God saw that it was good.

The Book of Genesis, chapter 1 and verse 25

In my back yard there are the remains of an old rubber swimming pool. It is one of those that has a big inflatable ring around the edge. It's developed a number of leaks, too many to find and patch; so this summer it sits flat and unused. At some point I intend to cut it in pieces and load it into trash bags to take to the dump. However, I have not gotten around to it yet. This spring it managed to retain a rather large puddle due to the frequent rain, making it a perfect spot for frogs to lay their eggs.

The water remained and the eggs sat there, giving me the chance to watch them over time as I walked by on my way back and forth to my workshop each day. As time went by, the eggs hatched into tiny tadpoles. These little fellows are perfectly adapted to swimming around in water. They use their tail to rocket themselves around with perfect ease. Of course, over the weeks little stubs began to develop that would soon turn into legs. For a while they are just useless things that tend to slow the little guys down as they swim through the water. Now maybe if the tadpole had a brain like us it would think:

"My God, what's happening to me? There is this weird change in my life that is slowing me down and making me look strange."

There the tadpole was, zipping around, enjoying life, and happy the way he was; perfectly adapted to his existing life. Then this change starts to happen. I don't know about you, but I hate change when things are going great and I just got happy the way things are. Wouldn't you know it, though, that seems to be just the time the Lord starts bringing things into my life that produce change!

Well, luckily for little tadpoles, they don't worry about these things; they just let the Lord work the way he intended to.

The tadpole lets God do his thing because those seemingly worthless stubs were in the process of turning into legs. Soon the tadpole is a frog. When the puddle dries up, the frogs simply use their new legs to hop off and find a nice pond or brook in which to live a happy little froggy existence. God knows what our future holds, and he brings the needed change that prepares us.

Carl Diener

A Predator's Plan

> Be sober, be vigilant; because your adver-
> sary the devil, as a roaring lion, walketh
> about, seeking whom he may devour:
> FIRST EPISTLE OF PETER, CHAPTER 5 VERSE 8

One of the fiercest enemies that birds and smaller mammals have in the woods is the fisher. It looks rather like a small, sleek bear with a long tail.

In the fall when small animals are out and about, gathering food to prepare for winter, God has made a natural warning system to help warn them of hunters. It's the thick blanket of fresh dry leaves covering the forest floor that crackle and crunch underfoot and make it almost impossible to approach prey without being heard, especially for two-legged hunters like me.

The fisher, however, is an extremely cunning predator, and I have watched how he gets around this problem. He uses what man has made to facilitate his hunting. You see, nearly all of New England was once farmland which became forest when farmers moved west for better land in the 1800's. The stone walls that marked the edges of the farmers' fields still remain, crossing the forest land. The fisher can run along the top of one of these walls, entering an area silently and unnoticed and approaching its prey to make the kill before the prey even knows what's happening.

It makes me think about the "runways" we humans make and allow in our homes and lives that make it easy for our enemy to get close.

One morning while deer hunting I had an encounter with a fisher on one of its silent pathways. I will never forget that day. I had sat down on an old stone wall on the edge of a stream. The morning was a foggy one and the stream and the stone wall were overhung by the branches of huge pine and hemlock trees that shut out much of the daylight. I turned my head slightly to check out the downstream section of the landscape. There was a deer trail that paralleled the stone wall, skirting the edge of a nearby swamp. I have had a theory for some time that I might be able to catch a deer returning to the cover of the swamp this way at daybreak, though I have yet to see one here.

As my eyes scanned the stream and deer path, I noticed movement on the stone wall where it emerged from the brush about fifty yards distant. In a moment I recognised the bounding, loping motion of a large fisher coming down the wall directly toward me. Discretion being the better part of valor, I should have perhaps stood up and let the critter see me. Reason told me that it would not be a good idea to stay motionless and let 25 pounds of bloodthirsty fisher land on my lap to see what happens. They are extremely fast and can take down an animal twice their size by ripping its throat out before it even knows it has been attacked.

Yet I sat as still as the stone wall, watching the oncoming fisher with fascination. The chance for a close encounter with one of creation's seldom seen and cleverest predators was too much to pass up. I waited with building excitement while the sleek brown killing machine came closer and closer. It was constantly scanning the undergrowth to the left and right for potential prey. It was ten yards away, then ten feet, then three. Still I sat without moving a muscle.

Then suddenly it spotted me. Motionless, it froze as if captured in a still photo, and so the image remains in my mind. I looked into those dark brown eyes and saw only the intelligence of a cold blooded killer. Perhaps you think it an exaggeration; but I have been eye to eye with many animals in my days roaming the woods. I know the gentle, intelligent curiosity of the raccoon, as well as the wide calculating stare of a whitetail deer trying to make out who or what I am.

What I saw in the eyes of the fisher that morning was totally different. I was looking into the eyes of death, swift and cold. It continued to stare at me for a few seconds, its nose twitching slightly as it attempted to confirm the identity of the being that sat before it on the stone wall. Satisfied as to what I was, it showed no fear but simply leaped lightly down off the wall, made its way around me, and continued its hunt as if I had never existed. Its thoughts once again turned to satisfying its insatiable hunger.

I have tracked the fisher sometimes in the white snows of winter in the woods and wild lands. I never have to track far before I find the blood of a kill. He is the perfect personification of our own spiritual enemy in his cunning and cold blooded cleverness. We should all be aware of the strategies he uses. Let's not give him any paths into our lives.

Carl Diener

Lost in the Wilderness

Thy word is a lamp unto my feet, and a
light unto my path.
THE BOOK OF PSALMS 119 VERSE 105

Out where we used to live in New Hampshire,
there is a wilderness area that stretches for miles. In
its center is a big bog. Not many people know about
this place, but it is one of the few true bogs in New
England. The water is so acid only hardy grasses grow
there and you find the strange plants you won't find
anywhere else, like the rare pitcher plant that catches
bugs for food. It can be a dangerous place to hunt in.
I once took a fall there on a ridge and busted a couple
of ribs. But as soon as I was able, I was back hunting
there again. It is such a wild and beautiful place.

It is also home to the black bear because of the
abundance of berry bushes. You can find places where
the big bears mark their territory by reaching up as
high as they can on the side of a beech tree and scrap-
ing it with their claws. If another bear comes along
and he can't reach as high as the existing claw marks,
then he knows the defender of this territory is bigger
than he is and he had better not stick around long. I
had an encounter once with a big bear in this area, but
that's another story.

There are places in the bog, as with most swampy areas, where you have to be careful because the ground may look solid but if you step there you will go under. I don't like the idea of dying that way. I can just picture the rapture: Jesus is waiting while a big angel rolls up his sleeve and with a disgusted look on his face he sticks his arm in the bog to feel around for Carl who is stuck down there. Suddenly his face lights up and he yells, "I found him!" and he grabs the scruff of my neck and gives a yank and I pop up with a giant sucking sound.

The bog area looks so similar in all directions and is so big that you can get lost down there on a cloudy, foggy day. This is bad because you don't want to be caught after dark when you can't see where you are stepping. I never used to worry, though, because I never got lost in the woods.

One dark, cloudy day, however, I was down in the bog and what never happens happened. I could not find my way out. Fortunately, I do carry a compass; so I dug it out of my pack and held it in the palm of my hand. The needle slowly pointed north and I began to plot a course to the east, where I knew the river lay, and beyond that the road where I would find my truck.

And so I began to follow that course, pulling out my compass now and then to check my bearings. It was then that a strange thing began to take place. Although I was sure I had entered the bog from this direction, nothing looked familiar. "This can't be right,"

I thought, because I have a knack for recognizing landmarks. I never get lost, remember? The further I went following the compass, the thicker and wilder it seemed to get. The terrain got rough and I had to detour around places that were unsafe to walk. This went on for hours and it was getting dark. I kept thinking that something must be wrong with my compass. I could see what looked like clear ways out of the bog that must have been the way I had come, because I was sure I had never seen the place I was standing before.

Several times I was tempted to forget about the stupid compass and trust my instinct. But then I would pull out the compass and watch where it would point. I would let out a groan; the direction east was again some patch of thick brush, or another ridge to climb. I was getting a bit scared at this point.

Just when I was in the thickest mess, however, it suddenly ended and I stepped out into a clearing. For the first time I recognized where I was. I could see the old logging road and the clump of pines beyond which was the bend of the river. Then, to my shock, I realized that I was only two hundred yards from the place I entered the bog!

It was then I heard the Lord speak to me.

"Did you think the compass was lying to you, Carl?"

Well, I guess that as dumb as it sounds, I did think there was something wrong with it, even though I know it couldn't be possible. The needle swung free and clear. Then the Lord spoke to me again.

"My word is like a compass that never lies. If you trust my word and don't doubt or lean on your own understanding, but follow it to the end, you can walk out of any wilderness no matter how deep."

Suddenly I began to understand how it was. I had seen people who were trusting in God's word for something and things seemed to get worse, so they thought, "Well, maybe this word is not for me." It's just like I was in the bog when I said, "Man, the way is getting harder, this can't be right." What the Lord is saying, I think, is clear. Stick to what he says in his word, and don't give up no matter how rough or strange things get. Believe and follow him and you will be all right.

Carl Diener

Tales of the Redtail

But they that wait upon the Lord shall renew their strength; they shall mount up with wings as eagles; they shall run, and not be weary; and they shall walk, and not faint.

THE BOOK OF THE PROPHET ISAIAH CHAPTER 40 VERSE 31

Spring is fully here now, and already on the beautiful sunny warm mornings the redtail hawks are soaring over the ridge above our house in the warm summer thermals. It looks totally effortless and, for the most part, it is; the warm wind keeps them aloft. They know just how to move their wings in the slightest way to take maximum advantage of the thermal as it rises off the ridge.

Suddenly, there is a slight folding of the wings and one of the hawks drops like a well directed arrow, gaining speed. About a yard before it strikes the ground, the wings open, there is a sudden final swoop with claws extended, and a snake is snatched from the grass and lifted helpless into the air. It all happens so fast, the snake never had a chance.

This is a sight that few people see, yet it happens all the time. What no one ever sees-because it never happens-is a hawk bobbing around on the ground in the grass like a robin. The snake might have a chance then. The view is very limited from the ground and the hawk's eyes were made by the Creator to see from far off. Bobbing around on the ground, the hawk would be quite vulnerable and he would certainly not be able to find and kill his food very well. God made the wind so that the redtail could soar high above his enemies, to lift him up so that he would be able to see the prey that God provided for him.

My pastor Dee likes to say that there is an ease in the glory. Jesus intended us to soar on the wind of his spirit and not hop around in this world praying that God would protect us and that maybe we will stumble into a blessing some where. God is merciful and he does often protect us and feed us in our stupidity. I of all people should know; I have been there.

Jesus would far rather, however, that we spread our wings of faith and soar on the wind of his spirit. Soaring high with him, we can see where our enemy is. We can see what our next move should be. God gave us spiritual eyes; they are eyes that can see things that we would miss with our hearts and minds tied to the earth. We can sense the wind of his spirit and rise with it. We can fly in the heavens with him.

Seeing that hawk soar away with the snake he just caught for his meal makes me think of a Christian who has been soaring in the heavens with Jesus and is now about to have the devil for breakfast.

Another thing about a hawk is that, like the owl I told you about, they are subject to harassment from the blue jays. I remember one morning hearing a flock of jays kicking up a fuss. I walked out on the deck and saw the jays diving on a perched redtail in the big maple tree in back of our house. The hawk simply spread his wings and flew. As he caught the rising thermals, he soon was carried far above the screaming jays. You see, jays can't soar. Their bodies are too heavy relative to their wing span. They just can't fly as high as the hawk. Soon the hawk was just a speck in the sky and the jays left the area, looking for other sport.

There is a place in the spirit where the devil's taunts can't reach us, when we soar into the heavens in worship, praise, and adoration of our God.

The doe that Knows me

And they shall teach no more every man his neighbour, and every man his brother, saying, Know the Lord: for they shall all know me, from the least of them unto the greatest of them, saith the Lord: for I will forgive their iniquity, and I will remember their sin no more.

THE BOOK OF THE PROPHET JEREMIAH CHAPTER 31 VERSE 34

Every winter around the fifteenth of December, I put grain out for the deer in the meadow behind our house. They have all learned that this is a place to find food when the snow gets deep and usually they come regularly at sundown in a herd of seven to ten deer. I put the grain out for them each day in the mid afternoon and space it out in small piles from the edge of the woods down almost to the garage.

In the evenings they come to the edge of the woods and stand there looking and listening before they step out to eat the grain. Often, herd animals find safety in numbers. While one is eating, another deer may be watching and listening for danger. Call it the herd mentality; we humans tend to be the same way.

I am sure most of the deer have no idea how the grain gets there every day, but there is one little doe that seems to have figured out that the scary man with the funny hat is the reason for it. Sometimes I see her watching and very often she is the first to come to the feed. The others run away if I should step out of the house for a moment, but not the little doe; she will stand and stare to see what I will do. When I step back inside, she goes back to feeding. As a result she always winds up with the most grain.

I sometimes think that the same things happen in the church. We get in a herd mentality; we are there when the meeting starts and leave when it's over. Only a few try to press in to God to know him and what really pleases Him, to understand his comings and goings. Only a few seek him early and then wait for him when all the others have gone back to business as usual. So many are content to come and get a little of God, just enough to get by on. Few step out of the crowd and take a risk. Few press in for more. Few find the real heart of God.

The smaller deer in a herd often get kicked away from the food by the bigger ones. Perhaps this doe was truly desperate. She found and got to know the source of the blessing, and as a result got more than all the others.

A God Given Rite of Spring

Praise him upon the loud cymbals: praise
him upon the high sounding cymbals.
PSALMS 150 VERSE 5

On nice days in the spring I like to go out on the deck first thing in the morning with a cup of tea and sit in the swing chair. You have to check the chair first sometimes, because the tree frogs like to sit there and blend in with the weathered-wood color of the boards. At night they jump up and stick on the wall of the house by the deck light and catch the bugs that fly around the light at night. See, it does pay to "remain in the light," even if it has you climbing the walls at times.

While I'm out on the deck I'll sit and listen to the woodpeckers drumming out their territorial challenges. Each of the males picks out his territory and finds a nice hollow tree trunk or branch that makes a good loud "tock" noise. Then he can drum out his challenge to the other males and let them know this is his place. You can hear them all over the hills in the early spring drumming away at each other.

One fine spring morning Laurie and I were awakened out of a deep sleep at the crack of dawn by something that sounded like a three-alarm fire bell. "Clang clang clang! Clangclangclang!" We looked at each other under the covers and both wondered what on earth that noise was. Well, it was a little male woodpecker drumming out his challenge on our chimney lid. I tell you what! You could hear it for a mile! The thing does not look at all like a tree trunk but somehow that woodpecker got the idea that it might just sound good to drum on. He broke with tradition of drumming on wood and found himself a heck of a sounding board. As far as I could tell, the little guy had the biggest territory on our road. Every morning for a week he would be up there drumming away loud enough to wake the dead for a good hour, right at the crack of dawn.

I remember one morning standing out on the deck, feeling kind of grumpy at being rousted out of bed every morning by the "crested land baron." I was looking up and watching the giddy little fellow up there dancing around on the chimney stopping every now and then to pound out a tattoo. I remember thinking, "A good dose of number 2 bird shot would ensure I get to stay asleep tomorrow morning."

Breaking with tradition will not always make friends for a person. Especially if one were to break with, say, religious tradition. Remember how much trouble Jesus got in, healing folks on the sabbath day? Seems like the church has never done too well with those that break with tradition, either. It's a sad history.

I could not bring myself to do any harm to that woodpecker. He was so full of the joy of living, carrying out his God given rite of spring in a newfound way. Oh well, what can you learn from a crazy little woodpecker anyway?

Carl Diener

The Fox That would not give up

And he said, Let me go, for the day brea-
keth. And he said, I will not let thee go,
except thou bless me.
THE BOOK OF GENESIS CHAPTER 32 VERSE 26

There are no open hunting seasons for big game in the late spring and summer. However, there is still varmint hunting for the sportsman who wants to keep in practice with stalking and marksmanship. In New Hampshire, that usually means hunting woodchucks. My father-in-law owns 50 acres of pasture and wood-land which just happens to be prime woodchuck habitat, so when Laurie goes down to see her folks I bring my rifle along. I've spent many years hunting this land, and I know where all the good woodchuck holes are and just where to sneak up on them for a good shot.

One sunny weekend afternoon I was crawling through the grass of the pasture toward the crest of a little hummock. I knew there was an active woodchuck hole on the other side. Once I reached the crest, I could peek through the tall grass for a view of the hole. If all was clear, all I had to do was slide the barrel of my rifle ahead of me and rest it on a clump of grass. I just had to wait until the woodchuck poked his head out to take a look around before he came out for his evening meal.

After about 30 yards of careful crawling, I came to the spot, checked out the scene and laid the rifle out with the front sight just a tad above the hole opening. I then laid back to wait for Mr. Chuck to make his appearance.

It had been a beautiful sunny day and on the crest of this little hill there is about the best view of the setting sun in all its glory in the whole town of Madbury. Not too far from the spot where I lay in wait for the woodchuck is a large flat rock where Laurie used to come and watch the sunset as a young girl. It was her secret place to come and be alone with God. I remember the first time she brought me there when we were dating. How special it was to sit there holding hands and watch the beautiful blaze of color and light in the western sky.

The sunset is a display that always reminds me of what a wonderful glorious god our God is. He paints the tapestry of cloud and sky with such beauty and majesty that no earthly artist could ever come close to doing it justice. Each sunset is a totally unique reflection of the infinite glory of our precious, wonderful God. Some people think it will be boring to be in heaven beholding him for eternity. No it won't! His glory and his beauty are like a billion sunsets coming one after another, hundreds of times more bright and majestic. It is a glory not only seen but felt as waves of pure infinite love.

Well, I was just stretched out on the grass enjoying the sunset when I saw a flash of red in the grass off to my right. I turned my head just in time to see the face of a red fox turn toward me not 5 yards away. We just stared at each other in total surprise for a few moments. It seems that both I and the fox had the same design of bagging a fat woodchuck from the hole just below us.

At first, it struck me as being kind of funny. I wondered how long we had been laying in the grass next to each other, so intent on watching that hole that neither one of us had noticed the other. Then, frankly, I got a little peeved. I now knew why the woodchuck hunting had not been as good lately. This fuzzy-faced dude had been hunting all my best spots.

It wasn't long before the fox figured he could not win an argument with me. He got to his feet and started to head out of there. Now the season on fox was closed, but the fox couldn't know that. A well placed rifle bullet zinging through the air between his legs would teach the rascal whose hunting ground this was, anyway. So I swung the rifle around and the sound of the gunshot echoed over the hills. The fox put on the afterburners and streaked out of there as fast as a fox could possibly run. So I got another round ready and settled the rifle down again, thinking rather smugly that I had taught the old boy a lesson he would not soon forget.

Soon the woodchuck poked his nose out of his front door. He looked around carefully, came out and started munching the nearest patch of clover. I waited a few moments more, took a deep breath and held it just as the sights settled on his chest. A slow pull on the trigger was all it took and it was over. The little guy never knew what hit him.

Well, it was time for dinner and I thought I would head to the house and have supper before I took care of my kill. I stood up and stretched my legs, and then I went in and ate. It was only about fifteen minutes later that I headed back out to the pasture. Yet when I reached the hole, the woodchuck was gone. A quick examination of the dirt outside the hole told me the story; the old fox had walked in after I left, grabbed the woodchuck, and took off.

I could not believe it. What kind of determination did that animal have, anyway? It must have settled in just inside the edge of the woods to see what would happen. Did it really expect that it had a ghost of a chance to wind up with that woodchuck when a human with a rifle was watching the hole? Yet at the end of it all, that fox's waiting had paid off. All he needed to do was walk in and take the meat just like it was a McDonald's drive-through. The close shave with a rifle ball hadn't deterred him in the least.

The Lord showed me something that day. It's a spiritual principle that you find throughout scripture. From Ruth to blind Bartimaus or the woman with the issue of blood, people received what they needed by perserverance. The lesson is clear: stick with what you know God has for you and don't be turned away. Maybe even the things that the enemy thought were his to keep will be given to you.

It was not long after that I made my first powder horn to hold black powder for the muzzleloaders I hunt with. On the outside I carved a running fox, as a tribute to a little guy that could not be put off from what he believed to be his.

The Bear Affair

Saying, if thou hadst known, even thou, at
least in this day, the things which belong
unto thy peace! but now they are hid from
thine eyes.

THE GOSPEL ACCORDING TO ST. LUKE, CHAPTER 19 VERSE 42

It's a very rare thing to get a big bear during the
hunting season. Yes, I know you can see them every
night at the Berlin NH dump, and my friend Bob Car-
ron has them come and rob his bird feeder, but I'm
talking about seeing a bear out in the woods where you
are allowed to shoot it. All us big game hunters dream
about it. The big bear rug in front of the fireplace, the
photo in the Valley News. You know, that sort of thing.

There was a lot of bear sign in the bog area where
I like to hunt, the place was crazy with wild berries,
and there was a beech tree where a bear had marked
his territory. So I knew there was a big bear around.
However, bears cover a tremendous amount of territory. They have many areas they claim as their own and
often travel miles in the fall looking for food. So when
I went out to the bog to hunt I did not ever expect to
see one; I was just looking for deer.

I was sitting there on a ridge in the bog wilderness in a thick patch of brush. It's not the best place to sit and watch for deer, because you can't see very far. Sometimes, though, I just want to sit and rest. It can be tough work clambering through the brush and I was tired and not really thinking about hunting. So I was just enjoying the quiet and beauty of the place when I heard some four-legged animal heading up the ridge through the brush toward me.

I was sure I heard four feet, but I needed to check and make sure it was not a person for safety's sake. So I carefully stood up. If it was a hunter or a person, it would be head and shoulders above the brush. I saw no head or shoulders. It had to be a deer; probably a doe, because I saw no antler tips above the brush. It would be coming out to the open very close to me. I lifted my rifle, tense with excitement.

Suddenly about 15 yards away the bear (because that's what it was) stood up on its hind legs and I was looking down the barrel of the rifle with the front sight dead on his chest: the perfect shot every hunter dreams about. For some reason I hesitated just for a second. But a second was all I had.

The bear, as suddenly as it had appeared, dropped down on all fours and took off at a dead run downhill. The old boy sure didn't hesitate when he saw me. I took a shot at a fleeting ball of fur when he came in sight about 60 yards downhill, but it was a dumb thing to do. The brush stopped the round. It was just as well; it would have been no fun looking for a big wounded bear in that thick brush.

It was all over; I had missed my big chance. I could not sleep at all that night. I kept thinking, "Good Lord, why did I hesitate to shoot? Why did I hesitate for just a second?"

Then it came to me: it was disbelief. For that one second, I couldn't believe what my eyes were showing me.

I wonder how many times it is that we hesitate because God came in a way we did not expect. How many times do we miss our answer to prayer because of our preconceived ideas of what it will look like? It ought to be harder to miss God than it was to miss that old bear, because God actually wants to be caught. But somehow the Pharisees missed it when he came. Let's not make the same mistake: let's watch and be ready for him when he comes.

Carl Diener

For this old Coon He died

And behold, they brought to him a man
sick of the palsy, lying on a bed: and Jesus
seeing their faith said unto the sick of the
palsy; Son, be of good cheer; thy sins be
forgiven thee.

<small>THE GOSPEL ACCORDING TO ST. MATTHEW CHAPTER 9 VERSE 2</small>

Spring is garden season. The last weekend in May,
most folks in New England plant their garden. For me,
living up in the pucker brush like I do, it's the start of
a summer long battle trying to keep God's critters from
eating everything I plant. This past summer I lost the
battle. The deer got in and ate everything. They even
dug up the carrots and ate them. This year I have put
up a higher electric fence to try and keep them out.

The coons were a bad problem in past years when
I grew sweet corn. I had to make sure that I ran
strands of electric fence wire close to the ground so
they could not get underneath the fence. The problem with that, of course, is that unless you keep the
grass and weeds trimmed down to the dirt, they will
grow up and short out the fence. Those darn coons
always seem to know when the fence is shorted out.
I think they stand outside the fence each night and

draw straws to see which coon is gonna have to touch the fence to see if it's working.

One summer I was busy and had not noticed that the grass at the back was all grown up to the level of the bottom strand of electric fence. A good rain and wind storm laid the grass over on the wire and that put the fence out of commission.

Sure as the sun comes up in the morning, the coons found out about it that night. The devastation they caused to my corn crop was a terrible sight to see. They pulled down every stalk and took one or two bites out of each of the ears and then went on to the next. It would have been one thing to take a bunch of ears and eat them and leave the rest for me. But no, they had to ruin the whole crop. It was criminal, horrible. I was so mad.

That day I went to see my old friend Wes and borrowed a cage trap. There was still some corn left half chewed, and I knew the coon or coons would be back the next night to make a meal of what remained. So I set the trap with a few of the half eaten ears for bait. I then cut away the grass from the fence and set the trap outside the fence. The coons would find the fence working and the only choice would be to eat the cobs I left in the trap.

As a hunter, I shoot game for the table and the fun is in getting the game. The killing really gives me no pleasure. However, with this coon I thought it would give me a great deal of satisfaction to pull the trigger.

So the next morning when I went out to check the trap I was elated to find a raccoon caught in the wire cage. Yet I could not bring myself to kill it. There is something seriously unsporting about shooting an animal in a cage, no matter how much of my corn it destroyed. Those little brown eyes in that cute coon face looked up at me with such a look of, well, help-lessness. There was that spark of intelligence in them. How could I do this to a little soul? Do coons have a soul? Funny how these sticky theological questions always come up before an execution.

Will the coon who is without sin cast the first stone, please.

Instead of feeding it a lead slug at high velocity, I think I actually gave it an ear of corn. Well, you know, a condemned criminal should have a last meal anyway. Then I thought maybe I could open the trap and give it a running head start before I started shooting. But the way things go sometimes, the little devil might actually get away and come back with seven other coons bigger and stronger than he was. Then the condition of my garden would be worse than it was in the first place. Seems like I read about something like that happening somewhere. So I left my death row inmate where he was for the time being, and went about my day. I still could not bring myself to shoot the little guy.

The next day I finally decided I had better do something about him. Late that evening I tossed the trap in the back of my pickup and headed down the road. After I had put a fair number of miles behind me I pulled into an old logging road, left the lights on and the engine running, got out, and pulled the trap with its inmate out of the back of the truck. I set the trap down in front of the headlights and opened the door. The raccoon hesitated for a moment, then ran out into the woods until he disappeared into the darkness, a free coon.

No doubt he still will find himself a corn patch. I don't think he was a repentant coon. However, I was fairly certain it would not be my corn patch that he would get into. I climbed back into the truck and headed for home.

A thought suddenly came to me. "What if, in order for that coon to live, I would have had to trade the life of my only son Sam in its place?" Such a thing would be totally inconceivable! There is nothing that could bring me to make a choice like that.

Yet that is exactly what the Father did. His love for us is inconceivable, unimaginable, unfathomable. He gave his one and only begotten Son for me. This old coon was loved beyond belief even when I was unrepentant. This old coon is forgiven. This old coon is free.

Carl Diener

Signs, Wonders, and Drinking Birds

.....drink, yea drink abundantly, O beloved
SOLOMON'S SONG CHAPTER 5 VERSE 1

One day soon it will become routine for the church to perform all sorts of signs and wonders. We will have finally caught up with God's little wonder workers, the hummingbirds. These little birds routinely seem to defy the laws of physics. They zoom in to the feeder for a drink at a blinding speed and stop dead in the air, hovering over the feeder opening. I think I once saw a hummer translated from one place to another and back again. This took place when the cat took a swat at one. When the cat's lightning-fast paw reached the place where the hummer was hovering, it disappeared for a moment, only to reappear in the same spot after the cat's paw had passed through the air.

The window screen in our bedroom was always falling out onto the front lawn in the summer time. For a while I wondered why. Then one day I saw it happen. Our cat liked to stretch out on the windowsill and sun himself in the morning. One of the little hummingbirds kept teasing him by hovering an inch from his nose on the other side of the screen. Finally, the cat couldn't take it any more and lunged for the little miscreant. The only result was that cat and screen landed on the front lawn while the untouched hummer hovered overhead for a moment before taking off. I'm sure it was laughing all the way.

While I think of it, I expect I have seen a hummer raised from the dead. I got out of my truck one day and left the door wide open for a moment. A hummingbird was flying around the house at warp speed and attempted to fly through the open window of the truck door. The problem was that he didn't see that it was actually closed. He hit the window with such a loud smack that I was sure the next moment I would see his dead body sliding down the window. To my surprise, he backed off from the window, hovered, then took off around the door as if nothing had happened.

You might not believe the next thing I am going to tell you; nevertheless, it's true. I had stopped by a greenhouse over in Vermont, just across the river in a town called Norwich. It was spring planting season and we had gone there to buy some plants. The greenhouse section that had all the flowering plants in it had about five or six hummingbirds inside, feeding off the flowers.

Well, there weren't any open windows in that greenhouse. The only opening was the huge greenhouse cooling fan that was turning so fast the blades were only a blur of motion. I couldn't understand how the hummingbirds were getting in, so I watched them carefully. They would hover for a moment in front of the fan, and then suddenly disappear into the whirling blades, appearing unharmed on the other side.

There is one more important fact about hummingbirds I need to tell you about. They could not do any of their amazing feats without getting a drink every few minutes. They are the creation's reflection of Jesus' wonderful offer for all who are thirsty to come and drink. These little birds are always thirsty for more of what they need from the Father's hand, whether it be from the flowers he made for them or the feeders we put out for them.

What an example for the church to follow. Always be thirsty, always be drinking from the source of eternal life: God's Holy Spirit. It's in our drinking and drinking deeply that we find the source of miraculous power and life. I love the way old Saint Augustine said it: "With the lips of our hearts we drink deeply from your fountain, oh Lord."

Sad to say, things didn't always go too well for the little hummers around our house. Just like in the church, there are those who want to control how much the others drink. Sometimes they even stop the others from drinking at all.

There was this one tough little male hummer who thought that the feeder we put on the deck was for him alone to drink from. He would chase off all the other birds. If they were particularly desperate and tried to get a drink anyway, he would fly into them at full speed. You could hear the crunch as his body slammed into the other bird in a kind of hummingbird hip check.

Well, what was I to do? I decided to open up another watering hole. I hung another hummingbird feeder around the corner of the house where old Pharisee Bird could not see it. Within an hour of hanging the new feeder, the air was thick with thirsty hummers coming in for a drink. They drained the thing so often that the sugar water was always fairly fresh because I had to keep refilling it. The feeder on the deck, on the other hand, got kind of rank under the guard of that male hummer. This was because I did not feel like wasting fresh sugar water on just one bird, only to have it go bad again because he was the only one to drink from it. Funny thing was, that bird kept drinking from the old stale sugar water. I guess he never even noticed it was going bad.

Carl Diener

Hart of Hearts Song of Songs

> I sleep, but my heart waketh: it is the voice
> of my beloved that knocketh, saying, Open
> to me, my sister, my love
> Solomons Song chapter 5 verse 2

I think by now I have established with some credibility that God does speak to us through his creation if we will listen to his voice. He also speaks through the creatures he has made. They tell us about Him, his glory, his majesty, his wisdom, even his sense of humor. Do you know what God talked to Adam about in the cool of the day? We all know it could not have been baseball! No, God talked with Adam about the things he had made. If you go to the book of Genesis chapter two verses nineteen and twenty, you will find that this is true.

In the Bible we see many references to creation that help explain the things of the Spirit and the wisdom of God. Solomon used many analogies from nature. If you remember, Jesus quoted Solomon's word about the ant, who has no overseer, but still works hard to put away food for winter.

Sometimes God shows us his very nature through the things that he made so that we will see and fall more in love with him. Jesus is the strong, all powerful lion, who is fearless and victorious over his enemies. He is the one who does great miracles and wonders. He is the one who will rule the nations. But he is also the sacrificial Lamb, gentle and kind, who gave his life for the sins of the world.

There is another way that Jesus reveals himself that you might not have heard people talk about, but it shows most clearly the intimate nature of his love; and that is the deer of the Song of Songs. In my precious times alone in the woods with my heavenly Father, I have gotten to know this side of Jesus very well. He is not only the Lion and the Lamb, but also the deer, our perfect Lover.

Years ago on a spring morning, I got up out of bed before dawn and got a quick breakfast. I then walked out to the truck and loaded my canoe in the back. This took a bit of effort because I have a heavy Coleman fifteen-footer. Part of it had to go over the cab of the truck. I finally got the canoe on the truck and tossed my fly rod and vest in and headed down the road. I turned off the main road and headed down an old dirt road into the backwoods. After a bit I found the old logging road I was looking for. I had learned about this road, and a beautiful pond that it leads to, by talking to a certain old guy who is retired and spends most of his time sitting out on his porch.

You can learn a lot from old guys that sit quietly on porches if you stop and talk to them a while. Most importantly, you need to listen. However, there are few people that will stop and talk, and fewer still that will listen.

The logging road was long and extremely rough. I had just begun to wonder if maybe I had taken a wrong turn at some point, when suddenly in the faint light of dawn ahead I saw a narrow patch of bright water. This was it! At least, the logging road ended here. So I got out of the truck and began the struggle to offload my monster canoe. With a little trouble, it was down and slid into the water. All that remained was to lay my gear in the bottom and push off.

It was the start of a beautiful day, as I remember; the sun was just coming up and the air was still and quiet save for the songs of the birds that were waking up to sing a welcome to a new day. The surface of the water was like glass and the canoe glided soundlessly out of the little cove into the main part of the pond.

I was sliding past a little peninsula of trees when suddenly the stillness was broken by a splashing in the water. When the canoe rounded the point, I looked around to see what had made the noise. What I saw was a scene that few people ever see.

There in the water was a little fawn splashing about as if it was the first time he had ever seen it. There was such delight in the way he pranced about, sending spray in every direction. Suddenly he turned around and it was then I saw his mother, a small doe, enter the water from the shore behind him. She was beautiful and graceful. The little imp dashed up to her splashing her with water, and to his great delight she splashed him back. It was a scene of the most incredible tenderness and full of the expression you see so often among God's creatures if you catch them in the wild and they are not aware of your presence. It's an expression of what I think is the pure joy of being alive in this beautiful creation that our God has made.

My friend Wes told me of a similar event he witnessed from high up in a tree stand. On a crisp, cold frosty morning in early fall, he actually saw a deer leap and buck and dance a little jig. This puzzled old Wes. There was no reason a deer should act that way as far as he could see. Well, I think I know what it was: a jig for joy! The beautiful words from the Song of Songs come to mind.

> Hark ! my beloved! Ah, here he comes,
> Leaping over mountains, Skipping over
> the hills. My beloved is like a gazelle or
> a young stag. Ah, here he stands, behind
> our wall, looking through the windows,
> peering through the lattices...
> SONG OF SONGS 2:9, THE BIBLE: AN AMERICAN TRANSLATION,
> SMITH & GOODSPEED

Like the deer is our beloved! He is full of life and full of joy! The world, especially the Muslim world, looks at God as one who brings death and destruction.

When it happens, "it is Allah's will," they say. Even our own culture considers natural disasters "acts of God." My friend, that is not the heart of our beloved Savior and Lord. He did not come to steal, kill and destroy; he came to give Life! Life abundant! Life full of joy! Joy like a doe and her fawn splashing around in a pond on a spring morning. The joy of a young buck feeling his strength and full of vitality in the early sunlight of a frost-filled fall day, at the first light of dawn.

Listen! Can you hear him, little child of his? Can you hear him calling you? Read the next verse:

> Rise up my friend, my beauty, and come away.
> THE HOLY BIBLE CONTAINING THE OLD AND NEW TESTAMENTS: AN IMPROVED EDITION, AMERICAN BAPTIST PUBLICATION SOCIETY

Rise up and come out of your humdrum life, your depression, your house where you hide yourself behind the walls you have built. Rise up and be filled with the joy of the life that he has to give you. Rise up and come away with him to a life of love and tenderness like you have never thought possible before.

There is still more to tell. The tenderness between the doe and young fawn that I saw was seen and understood by the writers of the old testament. Jeremiah 14:5 says that the famine and devastation to come in Israel would be so great that a doe would be forced to leave its fawn. The horror of the situation is clearly expressed. Only in the most extreme situations is a doe separated from the fawn. When you see them in the wild, they are almost always together. When they are not, the little fawn is always tucked away in a safe place nearby.

Solomon, who was a keen observer of God's creation, wrote about the most intimate characteristics in the deer. The tenderest reference talks of a young bride in Proverbs 5:19; she is a "loving doe, a graceful deer..."

I remember one morning when my Beloved came leaping and poked his head into the window lattice of my life recently. I was in the back yard by the door to my shop degreasing some old clock parts when around the corner drifted the smell of lilac. I smiled and dropped what I was doing, following the smell to the lilac bush around the corner of my house. I plunged my face into the fragrant bunches of beautiful flowers, inhaled, and then exhaled. I was praising God that he had made such beauty to smell and to see and enjoy, when the joy of the Lord hit me and I felt like dancing the dance of the whitetailed deer. Laughing, I staggered around the front yard for a few moments, totally overcome by his goodness, his love, his joy. It was joy unspeakable and full of glory! It's a good thing we live up in the woods; if someone had seen me they might have called the boys in the white coats to come and get me. (By the way, if they ever come for you, lift up your hands; it makes it harder for them to throw a net over you.)

The closer you are to Him, the more you look for Him; and the more you look for Him the more you will see Him and find Him, and the more encounters you will have with Him.

Talk to some hikers. Do they see many deer? You will find that most do not. They are out to see as much of nature as they can, but they do not often see a deer. If you want to see the deer you have to stop, be still, and wait. It takes hours, sometimes days, of waiting. Only as you remain quiet and watchful, eyes and ears open, will you see them.

I remember one time in winter I had walked out into the bog wilderness. There was no hunting season open then; I just wanted to be with the Lord and to enjoy his creation. I had sat quiet and still for many moments, when suddenly I saw in the depths of the woods a slight motion. I stared at it intently for many minutes. I was sure it was a small bird on a branch. In another moment I saw something else next to the bird, dark and shiny and round. I could just make it out. Then suddenly the bird twitched again, and I saw it was really an ear! I was looking at a deer ear. The dark shiny thing was its eye. Suddenly my brain put it all together. There in the woods I could make out a whitetail doe standing looking at me. She had been there all the time. If I had not been sitting there, quiet and observant and waiting, I would have missed this encounter.

In the stillness, in the quietness, He is there. Quiet your soul, listen and wait for him. He will come to you. I remember another time in the off season, when the deer were not in fear of being hunted, I had stopped on an old overgrown logging road while walking in the woods. Suddenly I saw two deer cross the logging road in front of me. Then a third and a fourth came into view. The third, who was a young doe, spotted me and stopped. I stood motionless, leaning up against a tree, and I watched and waited. The fourth deer also stopped to see what the doe was looking at. He was a buck, and he too stood still and watched and waited. The doe kept coming, nose outstretched, trying to sniff out what this thing was that was leaning against that tree. I stood without moving a muscle as she approached. She was almost close enough to touch before she finally caught wind of me. Only slightly startled, she turned and walked away.

I'll tell you a secret. I hunted whitetailed deer for four years before I even saw one, and five years before I ever got one. But slowly with practice and patience I learned how to be quiet, how to watch and wait. I learned the places that the deer liked, I learned to read the sign that had been there all along and yet I had never seen before. I learned how to spot the marks of a whitetail buck, the rubs of its antlers on a sapling. I got so I knew the habits of the deer and where to find them. I learned how and where to wait for the deer to come to me.

If you want to have an encounter with your beloved and draw close to the lover of your souls, you have to learn to be quiet; you have to learn to turn the eyes and ears of your heart to him. You have to learn to wait, and in the stillness of your soul, thinking on him, your spirit will be released to find him "browsing among the lilies."

Just like with a real deer, when you wait for him, when you learn where to find him, you will learn that nothing can stand in His way. No demon in or out of hell, no circumstances on earth, nothing can hold him. Truly he comes "leaping on the mountains."

If you should happen to meet me while I am out hunting you might see me headed through the woods, with the sweat pouring from every pore, as I try to make my way through the tangle and blow-downs that make up a true wilderness. Or another time you might see me trying to find a way up a steep ridge of a mountain. Suddenly you would see the flash of a white tail as a deer bursts out of cover, and in three or four leaps, it covers the ground that it took me twenty minutes to get through;

"He leaps on the mountains"!

I remember once I had found a place where a whitetail buck made its bed in the day in a small clump of thick sumac and brush. On two sides there was an open meadow. The backside had a strip of woods leading to a housing development, so I knew the deer could not flee that way.

With great care and about a half hour of careful stalking, I had the buck trapped. I was now at the end of the clump of trees. If he exited right, I would get a shot at him in the open meadow there. If he went left,

Ha! I had him in the open there as well. I knew he would not run to the houses. The buck was doomed. I had moved ever so slowly, but my scent must have got to him because I could hear him frantically dashing left, then right. But it was too late for him. I stood and waited. My venison was in the bag. Then suddenly he burst out of the brush right in front of me just yards away! He was headed right at me! I could not shoot; I was frozen to the spot. Help! In a split second he would be on top of me. Suddenly with one great leap he was high over my head. I turned around only to see him disappear in two more great leaps into the woods behind me. Our hero, the great white hunter, just stood there shaking like a leaf.

Oh yes, my friend, nothing can stop the deer of the Song of Songs. Nothing can hold our lover. Nothing will be able to catch him and bring him down. He stands on the heights looking down. He calls to you; will you join him? Will you let him make your feet like hinds feet on the high places? Why spend your life with your spirit and soul immersed in a mortal world where cares and worries weigh you down? Escape with him. Come away with him. There are places where he can take you; his secret places where others have never gone.

Have you ever seen a doe in the wild give birth? Well, you won't. The deer find a secret spot to give birth where no enemy can find them. It is a place so secluded only God knows where it is and only he sees. The Almighty God spoke to Job from the whirlwind. He ran down the list of things that no mortal man can do and no mortal man can see, and among the things he asks the terrified Job is, "Have you ever watched the deer give birth?"

Come away with him; he will show you wonders that you have never dreamed of. It will be a birthing place of great and mighty things that you know not of. Psalm 29 talks of the power and awesome glory of our mighty God. We see him shattering the cedars of Lebanon; he makes them skip like calves. They fly around like matchsticks in the force of his mighty power! He divides flames of fire! Then in the last verse, before every one in the temple breaks forth with shouts of glory, he says: "The voice of the lord makes the deer to give birth."

The blessing that Jacob gave Napthali was that he would be a doe set free that bears beautiful fawns. This is such a wonderful blessing. But the doe cannot bear fawns without the buck. It is only through intimacy that we will see fruitfulness; as we are set free to be with Jesus in the secret place he will birth beautiful things in our lives.

I don't know about you, but I want to be part of the bride who is intimate with the buck of the Song of Songs. I want to be found in the secret place with him, the place where his voice gives birth, the place that is only found in the heart of hearts. I want to be with him who leaps upon the mountains! I want to skip and leap for joy and live in the high places where the cares of this world cannot find me. Will you join me? Together we will find him in the stillness; we will train our souls to be quiet and we will let our spirits be tuned to his Holy Spirit. We will see him and know him and love him more and more. Then he will dwell in the garden of our hearts with his love and power, and we will radiate his glory.

Bush Fighting

For the battle was there scattered over the face of all the country: and the wood devoured more people that day than the sword devoured.

2 SAMUEL CHAPTER 18 VERSE 8

When I built my house, they cleared the lot first of all the trees and stumps. I could have had a great big lawn, if I had been a normal person; a nice lawn, pretty to look at, with a few well placed shrubs that would be pleasing to the eye. However, I like wildlife. You don't get wildlife with that kind of artificial environment. So I let the natural forces that God built into his creation take over. I set aside enough space for a small lawn and a vegetable garden and let the rest grow up naturally into wild raspberry and blackberry bushes, sumac, and black birch. In no time I had wildlife to watch and enjoy instead of a boring manmade landscape.

I have cedar waxwings, scarlet tanagers and most other New England bird species because they have food and cover on my lot. There are numerous small rodents, which means I can watch red tailed hawks soar above my house hunting for their prey. I also have the pleasure of seeing the great owls perched on my wood pile at night because they find the hunting here good as well. Yes, it looks wild and unkempt around my house, and some people look at it and see a mess. I don't see it that way. I look at it and I see life, wonderful beautiful life, bursting out everywhere. Glory to God! Then there is the added benefit that I have a wife who can bake the best berry pies in New England. All I have to do is walk a few yards across the lawn and pick them and bring them to her. Since I live way out in the woods, if I want to walk out in my underwear in the morning and pop a few berries in my bowl of cereal, I can do that too.

Oh well, I guess other folks get pleasure out of just seeing cut grass and an old robin hopping around now and then.

Like I said, I do have a lawn as well. While Sam, my son, was growing up, I needed a place to play soccer with him and teach him how to hit a ball with a bat. Now, however, I have the lawn because you are supposed to have a lawn I guess. You can't be a respectable member of the community without a lawn. Or let me put it this way: you can't look like you're a respectable member of the community if you don't have a lawn.

The problem is, it's hard to have a lawn when it is surrounded by life bursting out all over the place. Poor, weak, man-raised turf grass just can't compete with the wild plants. If I did not keep the lawn mowed and weeded, the wild plants would take over in a month's time. If I miss a mowing there are blackberry shoots a foot tall that pop up four or five feet out into the lawn.

I had thought that as long as I kept mowing, I would be winning the battle and I would always have a lawn. One day, however, I made a discovery that proved me wrong. I was sitting on the deck looking at the yard and I noticed that a tree seedling I had planted at the edge of the lawn two years ago was gone. I walked down and stared at the spot where it should have been. There was nothing there at the edge of the lawn but the blackberry bushes.

I was totally baffled. The little tree could not have died; it came from the north country. We had brought it back from a camping trip near the Canadian border. Transplanting it down here would be like taking a tough old desert raccoon home and taking it to Mc Donald's every day. It should thrive!

Instead, the little tamarack seedling had vanished completely, not even leaving the dead skeleton of a tree I would have expected to see if it had died. Where could it have gone? Trees don't just pack a bag and get on the bus. If they did, they would at least leave a hole behind.

I started poking around in the edge of the berry bushes and finally I found it; a little tuft of tamarack was peeking out of the blackberry bushes about a foot away from the edge of the lawn. How could this have happened? I began to look around. I remembered that there had been a rock hidden in the grass near the edge of the lawn that I would always forget about until I hit it with the lawn mower for the hundredth time. I hadn't encountered that rock lately, either. I hunted around in the bushes and sure enough there it was, now about six inches away from the edge of the lawn.

The bushes had been slowly taking over the back yard! How could it happen? I mowed the lawn every week, for goodness' sake! The mower cut off every invading shoot they sent up in the grass. Yet the bushes were somehow taking over. How could this possibly be? Berry bushes don't creep around after dark with evil thoughts about taking over people's lawn in the middle of the night. They don't just grow like crazy when your back is turned and then go back to looking all green and innocent and normal when you turn around and look at them. There had to be an explanation. I began to apply my mind to the problem; I suppose it's a healthy thing to do every now and then.

I pictured myself coming down over the dip in the lawn from the front of the lawn to the backyard, pushing the mower. I use the same mowing pattern every time. It's mindless work; I'm always thinking about something else at the time. So let's see, the first strip I mow is the strip where the berry bushes line the lawn.

And then I realized how the berry bushes were conquering the lawn. Berry bushes don't grow up straight like reeds or bamboo. They kind of bush out, and their prickly tentacles lean out over the lawn a bit. Here I come with the mower on the edge of the lawn. I get scratched a few times while I'm mindlessly mowing. The experience is slightly painful, and unconsciously, unknowingly, I shy away from the bushes a little, pushing the mower from the corner of the push bar away from the bushes.

I don't realize it, but that little bit of shying away from the scratch of those bushes leaves about a half inch of unmowed lawn at the edge. The next week, the same thing happens, and in that half inch of unmowed lawn, berry bush shoots are coming up. Three weeks go by and there is now new growth big enough to reach out over the lawn and give the old guy pushing the mower a painful scratch. The old guy then shies away a little and he doesn't notice that another half inch of lawn at the edge has gone unmowed.

Do you get the picture? Little by little, without my noticing it, the bushes had been winning the battle. They were taking over. I felt like the Lord spoke to my heart about this.

How many things are there at the edge of our lives that are a little uncomfortable and unconsciously or consciously we don't want to deal with them? Maybe there are things in our hearts that cause us pain to think about so we kind of just shy away. Perhaps we don't even give it much thought. We have so much else to think about or to deal with in our busy lives. How many people wake up and discover that there is a lot less freedom in their life, and they don't know why?

Well, now that I had solved the mystery of the creeping berry bushes I knew just what to do. The next time I mowed the lawn, I braced myself, reared the mower up on its hind legs and headed for the bushes. Chaaaarge!

Carl Diener

The Coming Of Elijah

And he shall turn the hearts of the fathers
to the children, and the hearts of the children to their fathers, lest I come and smite
the earth with a curse.

THE BOOK OF MALACHI, CHAPTER 4 VERSE 6

We had a cat once many years ago. It got sick and
we had to put it down. Our boy Sam, who as about
six years old at the time, wanted another one. So one
day, he and his mother went to the local SPCA to see if
they could adopt a kitten. Well, there were two black
and white male kittens who happened to be brothers.
Our Sam liked them both and Laurie had decided that
getting two cats would not be a bad idea, since they
could keep each other company when we were away.
The two kittens had names already for some reason,
and both looked alike except for distinctive markings
on their faces. Elijah and Scout were the names they
had been given.

I was still not too sold on the idea but it seemed
that in all probability I would end up going along
with the deal. For some reason we had to wait to
pick up the cats. I think it was because they were
too young to leave their mother just yet. Well, it

just so happened that the week we had planned to go pick up the cats there was a Revival conference in Vermont. The renewal that had started in Toronto in 1994 was just beginning to sweep over the world, and this was a general meeting of people and pastors in Vermont that wanted to experience more of what the Lord was doing.

We had been attending these meetings, and the day before Sam and Laurie were going to get the kittens we had settled down to hear one of the primary speakers of the conference. His name I can not remember now. He is nationally known I believe. At any rate, he got up to begin preaching and started off by sharing about how just before the meeting started, a little boy came up to him and told him that tomorrow he and his mom were going to pick up two cats. One cat was named Elijah and he had an hourglass on his nose and the other cat was named Scout and he had flames of revival on his nose. The guy thought it was prophetic or something. Anyway we wound up with the two kittens. How could I say no after some 800 people had just heard about it being an act of God?

The people at the SPCA said you should keep a cat indoors all the time. They even gave out a pamphlet explaining why. The world is a dangerous place, it said; cats can get hit by cars, killed by dogs, catch diseases and a whole bunch of other things. They finished up their little pamphlet by saying "Your cat will be happier and live longer if you keep him in the house." Well, I don't believe it. They might live longer, yet I know for a fact a cat would be happy to be outside if given a choice. Our cats had a choice and they generally wanted to be outside. Winter was the exception. The preferred spot to be in winter, of course, was by the woodstove or on the hearth rug if there was a fire in the fireplace. But for the rest of the year, people as well as animals were created to be out in the earth that God made. Nothing could be worse, in my opinion, than to be kept indoors all your life. My God, how horrible that would be.

The story I want to tell concerns Elijah, who was quite an unusual cat in many ways. As you will see he saw a good deal more of the wild woods then most cats will see in a full lifetime.

In the last 12 years since we built our home on the mountain (a hill to you people who live out west) I have never needed to drive anywhere to hunt deer. Our property is in prime deer country. So it was that on the opening day of the archery season for deer that year, I had dressed in my camo gear, taken my bow off the wall, and headed out the door. Once I had threaded my way past our apple trees up the old path to the ridge I began to walk carefully and quietly. I was already in deer country. I stopped for a moment to listen.

Immediately I heard the sound of an animal following me. I turned around and there was Elijah the cat. He came and sat down next to me as I was standing there. When I continued on up the ridge he tagged along. When I came to the place where I planned to wait and watch for deer, he settled down next to me. Occasionally he would get up and search for mice or stalk a bird. He always remained in sight of me and never strayed far away. When I headed home from hunting he followed me home again.

Well, this is extremely unusual for a cat. I don't think I have ever heard of a cat that followed its owner around like a dog. In fact if Elijah had been a dog, I would have been breaking the law. It is illegal to hunt deer with a dog in New Hampshire.

Elijah's habit of going hunting with me continued through the archery season. I was not worried about him scaring the deer away. Certainly when we were stalking through the wood together he made hardly any noise at all compared to me. When I made a stand on the ground he spent most of the time stretched out on the ground next to me where he could get his ears scratched and belly stroked. I didn't get a deer during the archery season that fall, but I'm sure it was not a result of having Elijah along. He was really an asset. If I kept an eye on him, he was very much an indicator of anything moving in the woods. His keen eyes and ears would spot any motion and his head would turn in that direction and watch. He could spot most of the wildlife around us before I did. Sad to say, none of the wildlife we watched included any deer.

The deep woods are normally a dangerous place for a cat, especially in my area. As long as Elijah was with me, though, he was not in any danger. One movement from me and any predator would have run. None of them would stick around with a human in the area. Even if they did not run, I think the shaft of a razor-tipped hunting arrow would have sort of impeded any designs they had toward making a meal of Elijah.

As you might know, cats are not like dogs. They are an independent lot. So, after a while, as I continued to head up into the woods in the early morning and in the afternoons Elijah did not accompany me any more. He just quit coming. I missed the little guy's company. On the other hand, I had worried about him sometimes when he came with me. If he ever strayed out of my sight it could go badly for him.

One afternoon a number of weeks later, I was high up on the ridge in a tree stand. I think it was rifle season by then, although I can't remember now. From way up on the ridge I heard the sound of some four-footed creature headed down towards where my tree stand was. I got the rifle ready to take aim should it be a deer, but the animal did not sound that big. Then suddenly, to my shock and surprise, I saw it was Elijah. It seemed he had taken to hunting by himself. To see him so far out in the woods did not leave me with a very good feeling. He trotted right underneath my tree stand on his way home and never even noticed me sitting up there. If I had been a fisher it would have been all over for Elijah the cat. A cat that travels on its own that far in the wild is not destined to live long.

I'm very sad to say that it was not too many weeks later I was lying awake in bed and I heard the howl of the pack. The coyotes were hunting the area. I knew in my heart it was the end of the road for little Elijah. Sometimes you just know these things. The next day Elijah was not to be seen and in fact we never saw him again.

I suppose we could have kept our other cat in the house after Elijah met his end in the woods. However, after they had tasted the life outside, the thrill of hunting, running, and rolling in the green grass on a beautiful summer day, how could we shut them in the house again for the rest of their lives?

Sometimes when I'm hunting or going for a walk in the woods I remember the little cat that used to follow. I miss him sometimes. I think about our own tendency as humans to be on the independent side. There are times when we just want to go our own way. Lately, though, I have come to a conclusion. My father in heaven has always wanted me to be free and to enjoy life and to have it abundantly. The big lie is that he wants us to miss out on the good things in life. Yet I find it is written that all good things come from the Father. I discover that my greatest joy in life has been those times when I have been with him in his presence. The most wonderful gifts I have been given, my wife, my son, have been given to me by him. The times I was on my own only brought a fleeting pleasure in the sowing and a great deal of pain in the reaping.

The days I spend with my Father, whether working, hunting, fishing or being with my family or friends, have always been the best days. And it is even more wonderful to have him by my side on the days when I run into life's predators. His lap is just a jump away and he is happy to have me there. The Bible tells us that our trials on this earth are temporary. So, just as the coyote and the fisher don't like to stick around when there is an armed human watching, the trials of this life just don't seem to be able to hang out or take much of a bite out of you when you jump into the lap of your Father in Heaven. The Bible also tells us that those trials are not worth comparing to the all surpassing glory that is to come. Sitting on the lap of the heavenly Father, resting your head on your beloved, is the surest way to make those temporary trials even more temporary. It's also the surest way to get a good dose of the glory to come while you're at it.

In fact, come to think of it, why wait for life's trials and predators to show up? Why not jump up into the lap of your Father in Heaven now. He is always glad to have you there.

It is written that the coming of Elijah was to turn the hearts of the fathers toward the children, and the hearts of the children toward the fathers. My hope is that there is a child of God out there that will read this story, and his heart would be turned back to the father in heaven who loves him and misses him so much. If this happens, then our little Elijah's coming will have counted for much and his death will not have been in vain.

To order additional copies of

REVELATION
from

Creation

have your credit card ready and call
1 800-917-BOOK (2665)

or e-mail
orders@selahbooks.com

or order online at
www.selahbooks.com